Scholastic Children's Books
Euston House,
24 Eversholt Street,
London NW1 1DB, UK

A division of Scholastic Ltd
London ~ New York ~ Toronto ~ Sydney ~ Auckland
Mexico City ~ New Delhi ~ Hong Kong

Published in the UK by Scholastic Ltd, 2016.

ISBN 978 1407 16583 7

Printed in Malaysia

2 4 6 8 10 9 7 5 3 1

Papers used by Scholastic Children's Books are made from woods grown in sustainable forests.

www.scholastic.co.uk

Welcome to the Disney Learning Programme!

Children learn best when they are having fun! The **Disney Learning Workbooks** are an engaging way for children to develop their maths skills along with fun characters from the wonderful world of Disney.

The **Disney Learning Workbooks** are carefully levelled to present new challenges to developing learners. Designed to support the National Curriculum in England: Mathematics Programmes of Study at Key Stage 1, this title offers children the opportunity to practise skills learned at school and to consolidate their learning in a relaxed home setting with parental support. With stickers, motivating 'Let's Read' story pages and a range of activities related to the film *Zootropolis*, children will have fun learning and practising their times tables.

This **Disney Learning Workbook** will help children to develop two important numeracy skills: firstly, being able to recall times tables facts quickly and effortlessly and secondly, to know how to use multiplication and division in practice. This book covers the two, ten and five times tables, as those are usually taught in Year 2, with the three times table being introduced in early Year 3. Some schools, however, vary this order and it may be helpful to check how things are taught at your school and decide whether your children are best consolidating what has been learned already, or whether there is scope to 'get ahead'.

Keep work sessions fun and short, and have a look at your children's work periodically so you can identify and help with any difficulties. If your children can learn the times tables by heart, by all means encourage them to do so: a one-off investment in rote-learning will pay off for years. But it is important to understand that some children find memorisation harder than others and can become anxious or frustrated if they cannot remember an answer, which in turn makes recall more difficult. Patience and support – and breaking down the memorisation tasks into manageable chunks – are therefore key. Aim to achieve the correct answer before speeding up response time.

Have fun with the Disney Learning programme!

Developed in conjunction with Chris Baker, Educational Consultant

Let's Practise Times Tables!

In this book, you will find lots of activities to help you learn and use some of the times tables.

Some people find it boring to learn times tables by heart but they keep coming up in maths, so a little effort memorising them is well worth it. It's like gaining a maths superpower! This book will show you that the times tables contain a world of patterns and that learning them can be fun.

- Find somewhere quiet to work.

- When memorising, work in short bursts, then test yourself to see what you can remember.

- Learn a times table thoroughly before going on to the next.

DON'T WORRY IF YOU MAKE A MISTAKE – EVERYONE DOES WHEN THEY ARE LEARNING! JUST CROSS IT OUT AND TRY AGAIN.

IF YOU ARE NOT SURE WHAT TO DO, ASK A GROWN-UP TO HELP YOU READ THE INSTRUCTIONS.

Check your answers on pages 44 to 47.

Little Judy Hopps grew up in a place called Bunnyburrow, on the outskirts of Zootropolis – a city where all animals live happily side by side. Judy believed the city's motto, 'Anyone can be anything!' with all her heart. At the Carrot Days Festival Talent Show she eagerly took to the stage and told the crowd that she wanted to be a police officer.

Suddenly, Judy heard a commotion. A young fox called Gideon Grey was forcing the other kids to hand over their Carrot Days Festival tickets.

"Gimme your tickets, you meek little sheep!" he snarled.

Judy raced to defend her friends from Gideon,
but the mean bully was too big. He pushed her over.

"Too bad no dumb bunny ain't never gonna be a cop!"
he sneered as he walked away.

Little did Gideon know that, while
he wasn't looking, clever Judy
had taken back the tickets.

As time passed, Judy held on to her
dream of becoming a police officer
and, as soon as she was old enough,
she enrolled in the Zootropolis Police
Academy. The training
was tough because
she was much

smaller than the other recruits.
But Judy was quick and smart
and worked harder than
anyone to achieve her
goal of joining Zootropolis
Police Department.

By graduation day, Judy
was top of her class. Mayor
Lionheart proclaimed
her Zootropolis Police
Department's first ever bunny
police officer.

Let's Learn the 2 x Table

Use a pencil for this page, so you can practise again and again!

This is the 2 x table. It's easy to learn.
Just follow the five steps in the arrow as you fill in the 'You try' column.

1. **LOOK** – look at the sum
2. **SAY** – say it out loud
3. **COVER** – cover it with your hand or a piece of paper
4. **WRITE** – write the sum from memory
5. **CHECK** – check your answer

The 2 x Table	You try...
1 x 2 = 2	
2 x 2 = 4	
3 x 2 = 6	
4 x 2 = 8	
5 x 2 = 10	
6 x 2 = 12	
7 x 2 = 14	
8 x 2 = 16	
9 x 2 = 18	
10 x 2 = 20	
11 x 2 = 22	
12 x 2 = 24	

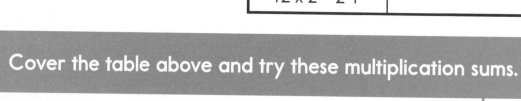

Cover the table above and try these multiplication sums.

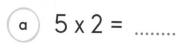

(a) 5 x 2 = ...

(b) 8 x 2 = ...

(c) .... x 2 = 22

(d) .... x 2 = 6

(e) 4 x .... = 8

(f) 10 x .... = 20

Finding patterns in a table can help you remember it.

> The answer to a sum is called a 'product'.
>
> For example, in the sum 3 x 2 = 6,
>
> 6 is the product of 3 x 2.

The 2 x Table

1 x 2 = 2	7 x 2 = 14
2 x 2 = 4	8 x 2 = 16
3 x 2 = 6	9 x 2 = 18
4 x 2 = 8	10 x 2 = 20
5 x 2 = 10	11 x 2 = 22
6 x 2 = 12	12 x 2 = 24

In the 2 x table, the ones' column always ends in 2, 4, 6, 8 or 0.

This means that a number ending in those numbers is ALWAYS in the 2 x table!

It also means a number ending in 1, 3, 5, 7 and 9 is NOT in the 2 x table!

Colour the numbers in this square that are the products of the 2 x table. The first two have been done for you.

1	2	3	4	5
6	7	8	9	10
11	12	13	14	15
16	17	18	19	20
21	22	23	24	25

Let's Count in 2s

Judy is hopping down the street, counting in 2s as she goes. Find the stickers to complete the pathway.

2

8

14

22

Let's Complete a Table Wheel

Complete the 2 x table wheel by multiplying the number in each segment by the number in the centre, filling in the boxes as you go. Two of the sums have been done for you.

Let's Play with 2s

Zootropolis Police Department has a very busy lost property room. You'll need to know your 2 x table to help out.

Draw a line to match each sum with the correct answer. When you've finished, everyone will have their missing items back.

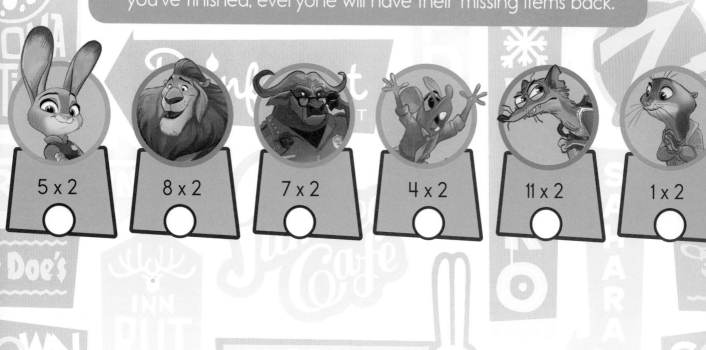

5 x 2   8 x 2   7 x 2   4 x 2   11 x 2   1 x 2

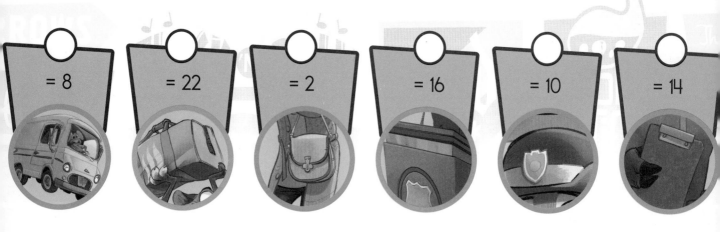

= 8   = 22   = 2   = 16   = 10   = 14

Help Nick and Judy through this maze using your 2 x table.
Place your finger by the entrance to the maze, then trace the path.

You may only pass over numbers that are products of the
2 x table, for example 2, 4, 6. If you reach a number that is not in
the 2 x table, you've gone the wrong way and must turn back.

START

FINISH

Judy loved working for the Zootropolis Police Department even though her first assignment was as a traffic officer. One day she was busy giving out parking tickets when a movement caught her eye.

A fox was acting suspiciously near the entrance to Jumbeaux's Café. Without a second thought, she crossed the street and followed the fox inside.

Jumbeaux's was filled with huge animals buying enormous dishes of ice cream. It turned out the fox was just trying to buy a Jumbo-pop for his son, who was dressed in a sweet elephant costume.

The fox, whose name was Nick Wilde, had forgotten his wallet, so Judy kindly paid for the Jumbo-pop. Nick's son, in his costume, reminded her of the time when the idea of becoming a police officer had been nothing but a dream.

"If you want to be an elephant when you grow up, you be an elephant," she told the little fox, because this is Zootropolis where, 'Anyone can be anything!'

Judy left the café feeling great about helping the foxes, but then she spotted the pair again. They were up to no good after all – melting the Jumbo-pop to refreeze into smaller ice-pops, which they sold to make money.

Worst of all, Nick's tiny son was not a boy at all.
He was an adult fox!

Judy had been tricked!

Let's Learn the 10 x Table

Use a pencil for this page, so you can practise again and again!

This is the 10 x table. Follow the five steps again to help you learn it.

1. LOOK – look at the sum
2. SAY – say it out loud
3. COVER – cover it with your hand or a piece of paper
4. WRITE – write the sum from memory
5. CHECK – check your answer

The 10 x Table	You try...
1 x 10 = 10	
2 x 10 = 20	
3 x 10 = 30	
4 x 10 = 40	
5 x 10 = 50	
6 x 10 = 60	
7 x 10 = 70	
8 x 10 = 80	
9 x 10 = 90	
10 x 10= 100	
11 x 10 = 110	
12 x 10 = 120	

Cover the table above and try these multiplication sums.

a) 6 x 10 = ...

b) 2 x 10 = ...

c) .... x 10 = 70

d) .... x 10 = 50

e) 12 x .... = 120

f) 3 x .... = 30

6 10 12

16 18 20 24

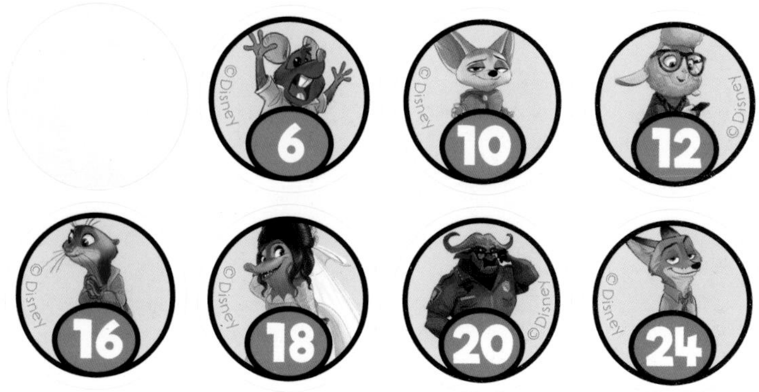

14   8   18   20

6   16   10   12

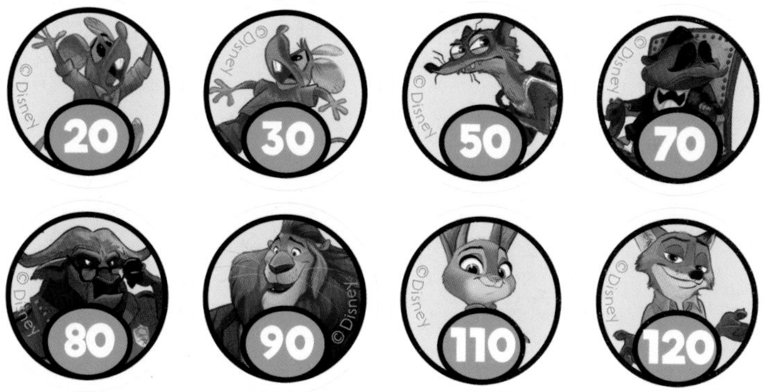

20 30 50 70

80 90 110 120

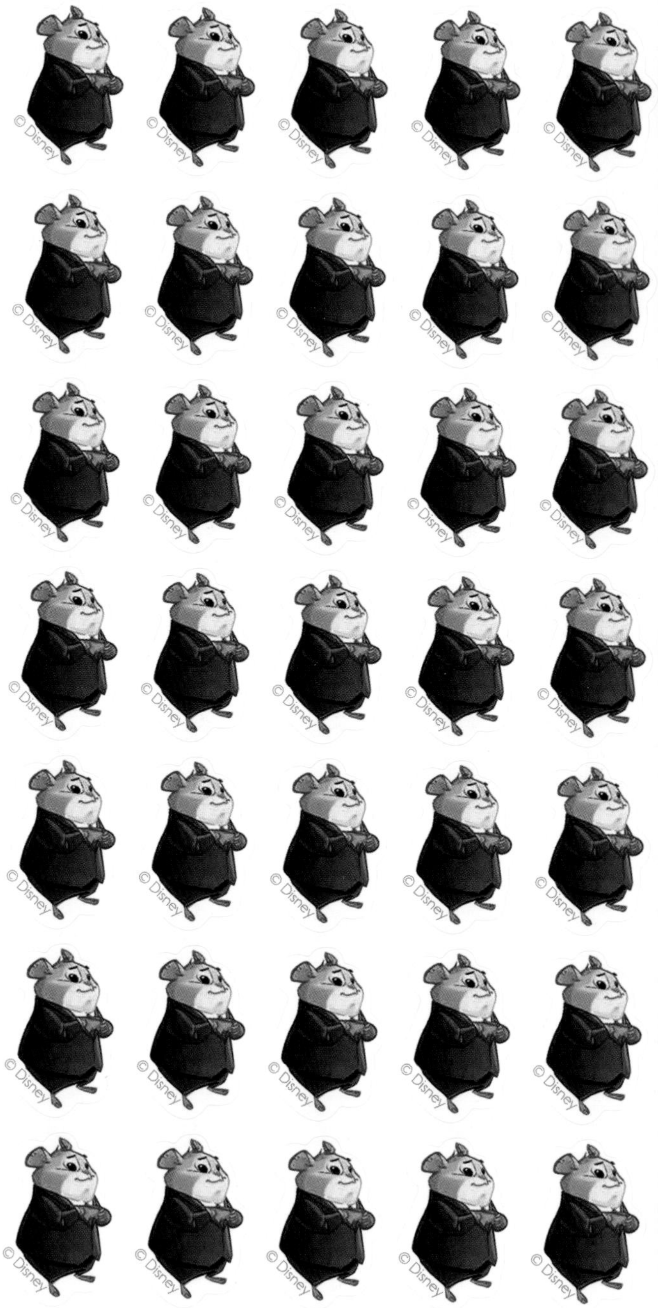

30p   20p   90p

50p   70p   40p

45   30   20   35

15   60   55   50

DISNEP ZOOTROPOLIS
© Disney

DISNEP ZOOTROPOLIS
© Disney

Pages 26–27

3   4   5   10   30   35   40   60

Page 32

3   9   12   15   21   24   30   33

Page 34

30 **15** **12** **18**

21 **27** **24** **9**

Page 36

J J J J J J J J J J

N N N N N N N N N N

Page 37

Pages 40–41

Let's look at the products of the 10 x table.

Remember, the product is the answer to a sum.

For example, in the sum 2 x 10 = 20, 20 is the product of 2 x 10.

The 10 x Table

1 x 10 = **10**	7 x 10 = **70**
2 x 10 = **20**	8 x 10 = **80**
3 x 10 = **30**	9 x 10 = **90**
4 x 10 = **40**	10 x 10 = **100**
5 x 10 = **50**	11 x 10 = **110**
6 x 10 = **60**	12 x 10 = **120**

Notice that the ones' column always ends in a 0.

This means that a number ending in 0 is ALWAYS in the 10 x table.

It also means that numbers ending in anything other than 0 are NOT in the 10 x table.

Colour the numbers in this square that are the products of the 10 x table. The first one has been done for you.

1	2	3	4	5	6	7	8	9	10
11	12	13	14	15	16	17	18	19	20
21	22	23	24	25	26	27	28	29	30
31	32	33	34	35	36	37	38	39	40
41	42	43	44	45	46	47	48	49	50
51	52	53	54	55	56	57	58	59	60
61	62	63	64	65	66	67	68	69	70
71	72	73	74	75	76	77	78	79	80
81	82	83	84	85	86	87	88	89	90
91	92	93	94	95	96	97	98	99	100

Let's Count in 10s

Nick is leaping down the street, counting in 10s as he goes. Find the stickers to complete the pathway.

10

40

60

100

Nick sells his Pawpsicles to lemmings for 10p each.

How much money has he made by selling:

a 3 pawpsicles?

b 5 pawpsicles?

c 9 pawpsicles?

d 12 pawpsicles?

There are 4 floors in the building. There are 10 lemmings working on each floor of the bank. How many lemmings work in the whole bank?

4 x 10 =

Complete the sum and then add stickers to show all the lemming bankers.

Let's Work with 10s

Help Judy find her way through Little Rodentia.
She should only step on squares that have numbers from the
10 x table. Colour the squares to find the safe route.

FINISH

14	33	18	91	45	100	110	120
51	88	41	11	22	90	15	8
96	29	53	8	4	80	66	55
3	64	12	36	70	38	21	27
16	48	72	60	24	17	56	32
6	30	40	50	93	51	5	78
20	9	24	19	2	82	1	13
10	98	39	7	56	99	61	49

START

Parking costs 10p an hour. How much
money should you put in these parking meters? Do the sum, then
use your stickers to add the correct fee to each meter.

a

4 hours x 10p

b

7 hours x 10p

c

2 hours x 10p

d

3 hours x 10p

e

5 hours x 10p

f

9 hours x 10p

Judy is writing down the number plates of
badly parked cars. Circle the plates that
contain numbers from the 10 x table.

a 29THDO3   b 30LRD09

c 110LRD07   d 71DWN46

e 80DWN100   f 96LRD674

Let's Learn the 5 x Table

This is the 5 x table. Follow the five steps again to help you learn it.

1. LOOK   – look at the sum
2. SAY   – say it out loud
3. COVER – cover it with your hand or a piece of paper
4. WRITE – write the sum from memory
5. CHECK – check your answer

The 5 x Table	You try...
1 x 5 = 5	
2 x 5 = 10	
3 x 5 = 15	
4 x 5 = 20	
5 x 5 = 25	
6 x 5 = 30	
7 x 5 = 35	
8 x 5 = 40	
9 x 5 = 45	
10 x 5= 50	
11 x 5 = 55	
12 x 5 = 60	

Cover the table above and try these multiplication sums.

a) 1 x 5 = ...

b) 6 x 5 = ...

c) .... x 5 = 15

d) .... x 5 = 60

e) 4 x .... = 20

f) 9 x .... = 45

Let's look at the products of the 5 x table.

Remember, the product is the answer to a sum.

For example, in the sum 7 x 5 = 35, 35 is the product of 7 x 5.

The 5 x Table

1 x 5 = 5	7 x 5 = 35
2 x 5 = 10	8 x 5 = 40
3 x 5 = 15	9 x 5 = 45
4 x 5 = 20	10 x 5 = 50
5 x 5 = 25	11 x 5 = 55
6 x 5 = 30	12 x 5 = 60

Notice that the ones' column has this pattern: 5, 0, 5, 0, 5, 0.

This means that a number ending in a 5 or a 0 is **ALWAYS** in the 5 x table.

It also means that numbers ending in anything other than 5 or 0 are **NOT** in the 5 x table.

1	2	3	4	5	6	7	8	9	10
11	12	13	14	15	16	17	18	19	20
21	22	23	24	25	26	27	28	29	30
31	32	33	34	35	36	37	38	39	40
41	42	43	44	45	46	47	48	49	50
51	52	53	54	55	56	57	58	59	60
61	62	63	64	65	66	67	68	69	70
71	72	73	74	75	76	77	78	79	80
81	82	83	84	85	86	87	88	89	90
91	92	93	94	95	96	97	98	99	100

Colour the numbers in this square that are the products of the 5 x table. The first one has been done for you.

Something strange is happening in Zootropolis. Five animals are turning savage each day. Use your stickers to add the numbers of savage animals onto the diary pages.

ZPD

Zootropolis Police Department

Diary

Monday	Tuesday	Wednesday	Thursday	Friday	Saturday	Sunday
5	10					
Monday	Tuesday	Wednesday	Thursday	Friday	Saturday	Sunday
				25		
40						
Monday	Tuesday	Wednesday	Thursday	Friday	Saturday	Sunday
						CASE SOLVED

NIGHT HOWLER FILE

Choose the correct answer for each sum.
Colour the letter next to that answer.

a   3 x 5 = 12? **W**   OR = 15? **H**

b   7 x 5 = 35? **O**   OR = 30? **I**

c   12 x 5 = 55? **L**   OR = 60? **P**

d   8 x 5 = 48? **E**   OR = 40? **P**

e   4 x 5 = 20? **S**   OR = 25? **N**

The letters you have coloured spell a **Zootropolis** character's surname.
Write it in the space below.

_____ _____ _____ _____ _____ _____

a The Zootropolis florist shop has 2 big windows. Each window holds 5 pots of flowers. How many pots are in the shop's windows altogether?

☐ X ☐ = ☐

b Each police parking vehicle carries 3 traffic cones. There are 5 police parking vehicles on the streets today. How many traffic cones are they carrying in total?

☐ X ☐ = ☐

c Kevin the Polar Bear stops 7 animals from seeing Mr Big every hour. He has been at work for 5 hours. How many people has Kevin stopped from seeing Mr Big?

☐ X ☐ = ☐

Let's Visit Mystic Spring Oasis

A visit to the Mystic Spring Oasis makes you five times more happy.

How happy were these characters before or after their visit? Fill in the blanks.

Happiness before [12] 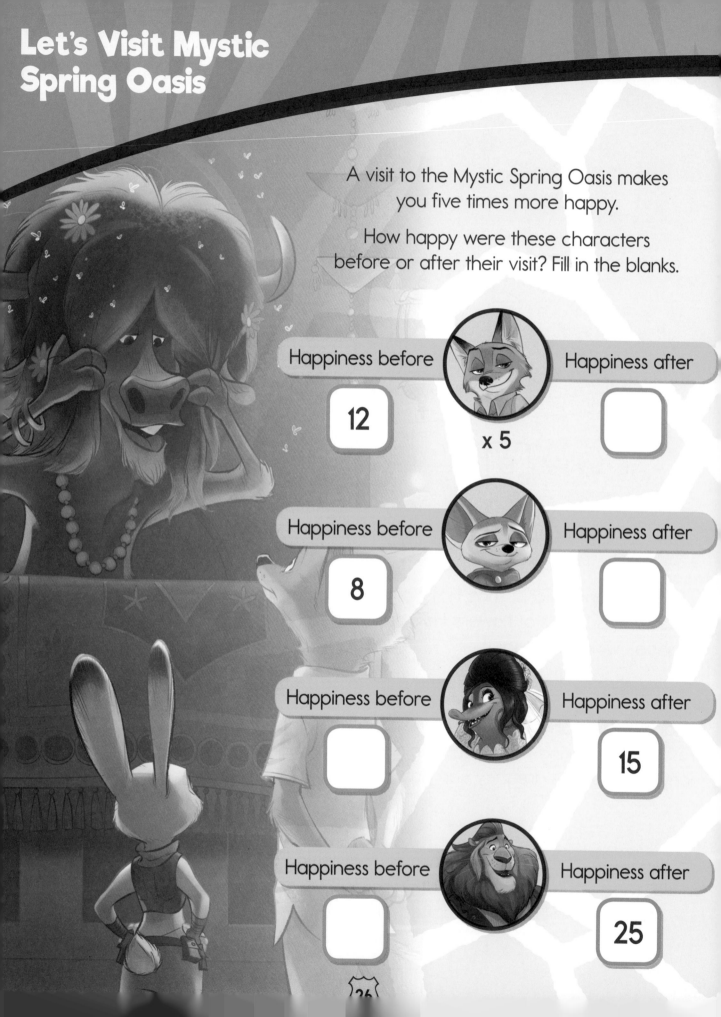 x 5 Happiness after [ ]

Happiness before [8] Happiness after [ ]

Happiness before [ ] Happiness after [15]

Happiness before [ ] Happiness after [25]

Doing yoga at Mystic Spring Oasis makes you five times less tired.

How tired were these characters before or after their visit? Fill in the blanks.

Tiredness before

Tiredness after

20

÷ 5

Tiredness before

Tiredness after

50

Tiredness before

Tiredness after

7

Tiredness before

Tiredness after

6

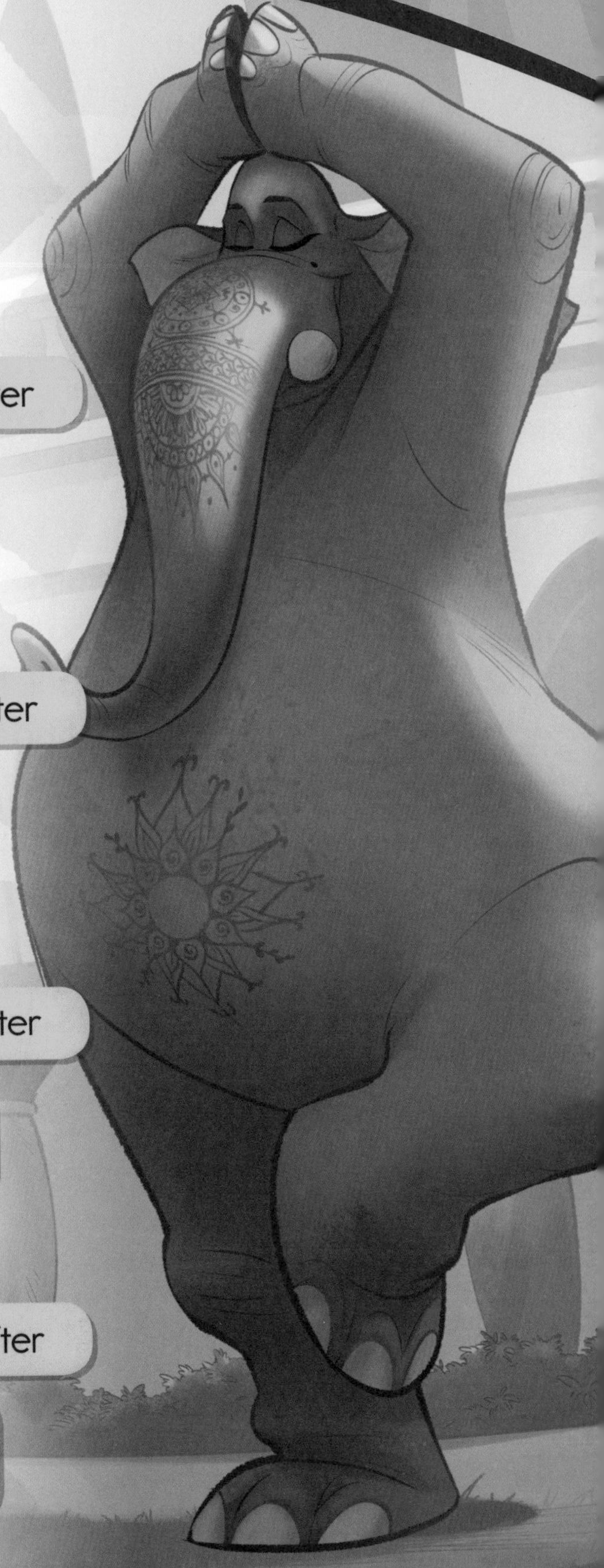

Police Officer Judy Hopps finally got her first real police assignment. She was in Chief Bogo's office when Mrs Otterton burst in to report her husband, Emmitt, missing. Judy offered to help and Assistant Mayor Bellwether unexpectedly agreed she should take the case.

In the Otterton file Judy noticed a photo of Emmitt buying an ice-pop from Nick Wilde! She tracked down the fox and his pal, Finnick and tricked Nick into helping her by recording his boasting about his crimes. She threatened him with prison unless he took her to where he had last seen the otter.

The trail took them all over Zootropolis, from the Mystic Springs Oasis to Tundratown, where they met crime boss, Mr Big. They ended up in the Rainforest District looking for Mr Big's driver, Manchas the jaguar, who was the last person to have seen Emmitt.

Manchas was terrified. He had been attacked by the otter.

"He was down on all fours, a savage," Manchas said. "There was no warning. He just kept yelling about night howlers."

Suddenly, Manchas turned savage. Judy and Nick escaped from the crazed jaguar, but only just in time. The case had taken a shocking turn. What were 'night howlers'? Why were animals turning savage?

Nick and Judy would have to work together to find out!

Let's Learn the 3 x Table

Use a pencil for this page, so you can practise again and again!

This is the 3 x table. Follow the five steps to help you learn it.

1. LOOK – look at the sum
2. SAY – say it out loud
3. COVER – cover it with your hand or a piece of paper
4. WRITE – write the sum from memory
5. CHECK – check your answer

The 3 x Table	You try ...
1 x 3 = 3	
2 x 3 = 6	
3 x 3 = 9	
4 x 3 = 12	
5 x 3 = 15	
6 x 3 = 18	
7 x 3 = 21	
8 x 3 = 24	
9 x 3 = 27	
10 x 3 = 30	
11 x 3 = 33	
12 x 3 = 36	

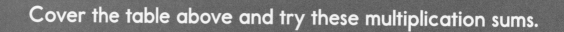

Cover the table above and try these multiplication sums.

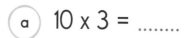

(a) 10 x 3 = ...

(b) 5 x 3 = ...

(c) .... x 3 = 24

(d) .... x 3 = 27

(e) 12 x .... = 36

(f) 6 x .... = 18

Let's look at the products of the 3 x table.

Remember, the product is the answer to a sum.

For example, in the sum 11 x 3 = 33, 33 is the product of 11 x 3.

The pattern starts 3, 6 and 9 but then appears to change.

In fact, the pattern continues. If you add up the digits in the products from 4 x 3 onwards, you will always get 3, 6 or 9.

In 4 x 3 = 12, adding the 1 and the 2 = 3.
In 5 x 3 = 15, adding the 1 and the 5 = 6.

The 3 x Table

1 x 3 = 3	7 x 3 = 21
2 x 3 = 6	8 x 3 = 24
3 x 3 = 9	9 x 3 = 27
4 x 3 = 12	10 x 3 = 30
5 x 3 = 15	11 x 3 = 33
6 x 3 = 18	12 x 3 = 36

Adding the last two digits of a number together to check they make either 3, 6 or 9, is a good way to make sure a number is in the 3 x table.

Colour the numbers in this square that are the products of the 3 x table. The first one has been done for you.

1	2	3	4	5	6	7	8	9	10
11	12	13	14	15	16	17	18	19	20
21	22	23	24	25	26	27	28	29	30
31	32	33	34	35	36	37	38	39	40
41	42	43	44	45	46	47	48	49	50
51	52	53	54	55	56	57	58	59	60
61	62	63	64	65	66	67	68	69	70
71	72	73	74	75	76	77	78	79	80
81	82	83	84	85	86	87	88	89	90
91	92	93	94	95	96	97	98	99	100

Let's Count in 3s

Mr and Mrs Hopps are picking flowers on their farm. They pull them up 3 at a time. Stick the right number under the sets of flowers.

Help Judy and Nick to open the safe
by completing the sums on the clue sheet.
Write the numbers left to right in the safe window.

SAFE CRACKER CLUE SHEET

3 x 3 = ...

11 x .... = 33

7 x 3 = ...

.... x 3 = 15

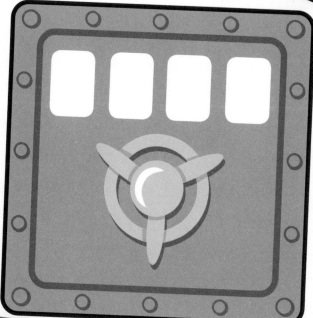

Together the numbers on 3 of these test tubes
make a sum from the 3 x table. Which three?

Write the sum out in the space below.

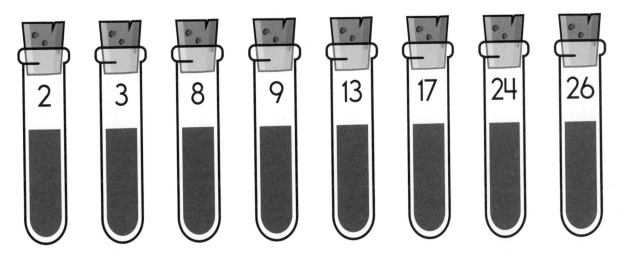

2   3   8   9   13   17   24   26

.... X .... = ...

Let's Complete a Table Wheel

Complete the 3 x table wheel by multiplying the number in each segment by the number in the centre, filling in the boxes as you go. Two examples have been done for you.

3

6

x3

10 1

9   2

8   3

7   4

6   5

Police officers like Judy need lightning-quick reactions. Train your brain with this 3 x table quick quiz. Use a pencil so you can rub out the answers and try again.

a 3 x 3 =

b 7 x 3 =

c What is six multiplied by three?

d ☐ x 3 = 12

e 10 x 3 =

f 33 = ☐ x 3

g 27 = ☐ x 3

h Multiply 2 by 3

i 8 x 3 =

k What are the first six answers to the 3 x table?

j ☐ x 3 = 36

Let's Practise Mixed Tables

Judy and Nick have to search 21 houses in this street. Nick will search all the houses with numbers in the 3 x table. Judy will search all of the houses with numbers in the 2 x table.

Put an N sticker on the houses Nick will search, and a J sticker on the houses Judy will search.

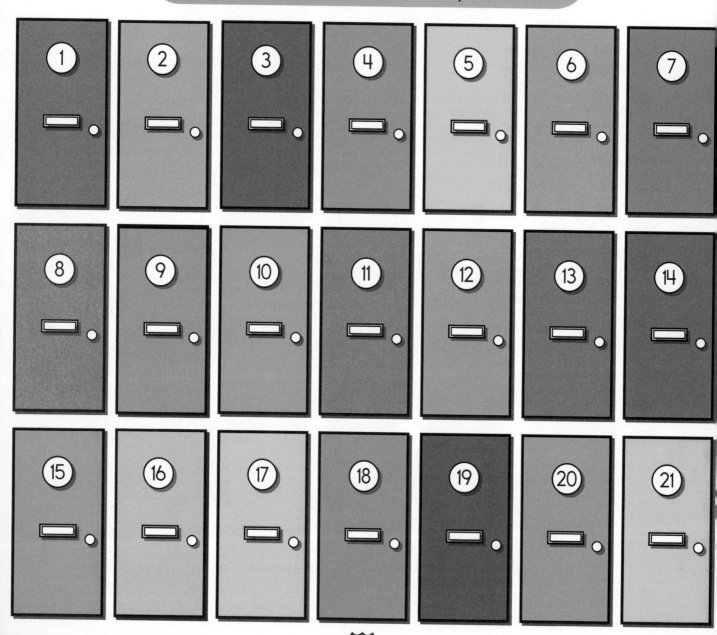

Can you answer these questions?

a) Which houses would Nick search?

b) Which houses would Judy search?

c) Who would search more houses?

d) Are there any houses they would both search? If so, which?

e) Are there any houses that won't get searched? If so, which?

f) Would this be a good way to share the work? Would the job get done properly?

Write your answers here

a) ....

b) ....

c) ....

d) ....

e) ....

f) ....

Which bottle contains the night howler pellet? Use these clues to find out, and put the sticker with the cross on the right bottle.

The night howler bottle has a number that is:

- in the 2 x table
- more than 12
- in the 3 x table

Now use these clues to find which bottle contains blueberries. Put the blueberry sticker on the right bottle.

2   7   12   15   24   33   35   40

The blueberry bottle has a number that is NOT in the:

- 2 x table
- 10 x table
- 5 x table
- 3 x table

Let's Make It

Practise your times tables while making cool friendship bracelets for you and your best buddy!

You will need:

- 60 beads – 20 each of 3 different colours
- 9 small pots
- 40 cm length of elastic
- a pair of scissors

To make 2 bracelets, you will need 6 sets of 10 beads, in 3 different colours.

Can you write a multiplication sum to show how many beads you need in total?

What you do:

a First sort the beads into colour groups.

Write the colours into the table below:

Colour A	
Colour B	
Colour C	

Scissors are sharp! Ask a grown-up to help with this craft.

b Pick out 6 Colour A beads.

How many pots will you need, if you put 3 beads in each? ☐

c Take 5 more pots. Put 2 Colour B beads in each.

How many Colour B beads will you need to pick out in total? ☐

d Pick out 8 Colour C beads. Sort them equally into 2 pots.

How many beads will be in each pot? ☐

e Take the elastic, fold it in half and cut it into 2 equal pieces.

How long will each piece need to be? $2 \times ? = 40$ ☐ cm

f Now for the fun part! Take one piece of elastic. Tie a knot at one end. Thread on all of the beads from the 9 pots, in any order you like.

g Tie a knot after the last bead to hold the beads in place. Now ask your grown-up helper to fit your bracelet by wrapping the elastic around your wrist and cutting off any excess. They can remove one or two beads if necessary. Now tie the two ends together in a knot.

Once you have finished your bracelet repeat steps b to g to make a bracelet for your friend!

Here Are All the Things I Can Do

Put a Zootropolis sticker next to the things that you can do!

I can remember...

the 2 x table

the 10 x table

the 5 x table

the 3 x table

I can count in...

2s

10s

5s

3s

I know a pattern that tells me whether...

a number is in the 2 x table

a number is in the 10 x table

a number is in the 5 x table

a number is in the 3 x table

I can complete...

a multiplication wheel

I can confidently...

work with mixed tables

use tables within a craft activity

Find opportunities to use tables

Help your child to see that times tables really do turn up everywhere, so that learning them is worthwhile. Point out instances when you or other family members use tables and let your child use their knowledge to help – for example:

- in cooking (how long is the cooking time? How many eggs?)
- in craft or DIY projects (how many floor tiles? How much paint or cement or other materials will we need?)
- at the table (how many biscuits each?)
- in sport (what does our team need to do in order to win?)

Times tables turn up in many games and sports. Rugby Union, for example, awards 5 points for a try, 2 points for a conversion and 3 points for a penalty, so it is perfect for using knowledge of the 5, 3 and 2 times tables.

The right support

If you can, find your child somewhere quiet to work. Short, concentrated bursts of memorisation often work better than long ones when your child may get bored. Stop before your child is tired and dispirited. Switch between different kinds of practice to help keep things fresh. Like most worthwhile skills, learning tables takes time to acquire. Help your child to keep working at it regularly. Think of it as a kind of 'maths fitness'.

Be positive about learning maths! Unfortunately, some adults had a bad time in maths lessons at school. If that's true of you or your family, try not to give your child the impression that maths is boring, difficult or geeky as there is a risk your child will believe you and give up.

Praise good efforts!

Some children can memorise the tables quickly and easily. Others, just as intelligent, find it takes them much longer. Praise your child for their efforts and make sure they know you value hard work.

Answers

Pages 8–9

a) 10
b) 16
c) 11
d) 3
e) 2
f) 2

1	2	3	4	5
6	7	8	9	10
11	12	13	14	15
16	17	18	19	20
21	22	23	24	25

Pages 16–17

a) 60   d) 5
b) 20   e) 10
c) 7   f) 10

1	2	3	4	5	6	7	8	9	10
11	12	13	14	15	16	17	18	19	20
21	22	23	24	25	26	27	28	29	30
31	32	33	34	35	36	37	38	39	40
41	42	43	44	45	46	47	48	49	50
51	52	53	54	55	56	57	58	59	60
61	62	63	64	65	66	67	68	69	70
71	72	73	74	75	76	77	78	79	80
81	82	83	84	85	86	87	88	89	90
91	92	93	94	95	96	97	98	99	100

Page 10

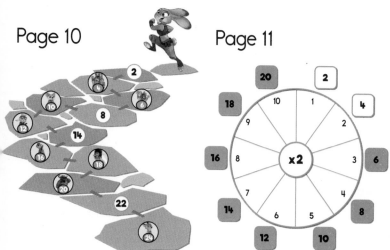

Page 11

Page 12

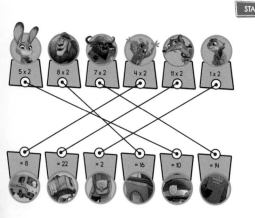

Page 13

Page 18

Page 19

a) 30p
b) 50p
c) 90p
d) 120p (£1.20)

40 lemmings work in the bank altogether: 4 x 10 = 40

Page 20

14	33	18	91	45	100	110	120
51	88	41	11	22	90	15	8
96	29	53	8	4	80	66	55
3	64	12	36	70	38	21	27
16	48	72	60	24	17	56	32
6	30	40	50	93	51	5	78
20	9	24	19	2	82	1	13
10	98	39	7	56	99	61	49

Page 21

a) 40p
b) 70p
c) 20p
d) 30p
e) 50p
f) 90p

Number plate puzzle:
b), c) and e) contain
numbers from the 10 x table.

Pages 22–23

a) 5   d) 12
b) 30   e) 5
c) 3   f) 5

1	2	3	4	5	6	7	8	9	10
11	12	13	14	15	16	17	18	19	20
21	22	23	24	25	26	27	28	29	30
31	32	33	34	35	36	37	38	39	40
41	42	43	44	45	46	47	48	49	50
51	52	53	54	55	56	57	58	59	60
61	62	63	64	65	66	67	68	69	70
71	72	73	74	75	76	77	78	79	80
81	82	83	84	85	86	87	88	89	90
91	92	93	94	95	96	97	98	99	100

Page 24

Monday	Tuesday	Wednesday	Thursday	Friday	Saturday	Sunday
5	10	15	20	25	30	35
Monday	Tuesday	Wednesday	Thursday	Friday	Saturday	Sunday
40	45	50	55	60	CASE SOLVED	

Page 25

a) 15   b) 35   c) 60   d) 40   e) 20

Shaded name: H O P P S

a) 2 x 5 = 10
b) 3 x 5 = 15
c) 7 x 5 = 35

Answers

Pages 26–27

 Happiness after = 60

 Happiness after = 40

 Happiness before = 3

 Happiness before = 5

 Tiredness after = 4

 Tiredness after = 10

 Tiredness before = 35

Tiredness before = 30

Pages 30–31

a) 30   d) 9
b) 15   e) 3
c) 8   f) 3

1	2	3	4	5	6	7	8	9	10
11	12	13	14	15	16	17	18	19	20
21	22	23	24	25	26	27	28	29	30
31	32	33	34	35	36	37	38	39	40
41	42	43	44	45	46	47	48	49	50
51	52	53	54	55	56	57	58	59	60
61	62	63	64	65	66	67	68	69	70
71	72	73	74	75	76	77	78	79	80
81	82	83	84	85	86	87	88	89	90
91	92	93	94	95	96	97	98	99	100

Page 32

3 6 9 12
15 18 21 24
27 30 33 36

Page 33

The safe combination: 9, 3, 21, 5
Test tube sum: 3 x 8 = 24

Page 34

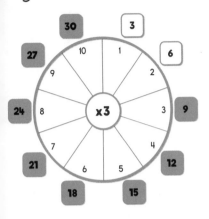

Page 35

a) 9   f) 11
b) 21   g) 9
c) 18   h) 6
d) 4   i) 24
e) 30   j) 12

k) 3; 6; 9; 12; 15; 18.

Page 37

a) Nick will search houses 3, 6, 9, 12, 15, 18 and 21.

b) Judy will search houses 2, 4, 6, 8, 10, 12, 14, 16, 18 and 20.

c) Judy. She would search 10 houses, Nick would only search 7.

d) They would both search houses 6, 12 and 18.

e) The houses that won't get searched are 1, 5, 7, 11, 13, 17 and 19.

f) No. Work is not shared out fairly; some houses are searched twice and others not at all.

Page 37

 Bottle 7 contains the blueberries.

 Bottle 24 is the night howler poison.

Pages 38–39

b) 2
c) 10
d) 4
e) 20 cm

CONGRATULATIONS!

....

(Name)

**has completed the
Disney Learning Workbook:**

TIMES TABLES

Presented on

....

(Date)

....

(Parent's Signature)

Disney ZOOTROPOLIS